I0803719

My State IOWA

By Christina Earley

TABLE OF CONTENTS

A Crabtree Seedlings Book

Crabtree Publishing

crabtreebooks.com

School-to-Home Support for Caregivers and Teachers

This book helps children grow by letting them practice reading. Here are a few guiding questions to help the reader build his or her comprehension skills. Possible answers appear in red.

Before Reading:

- What do I know about Iowa?
    - *I know that Iowa is a state.*
    - *I know that Iowa grows a lot of corn.*

- What do I want to learn about Iowa?
    - *I want to learn which famous people were born in Iowa.*
    - *I want to learn what the state flag looks like.*

During Reading:

- What have I learned so far?
    - *I have learned that Des Moines is the state capital of Iowa.*
    - *I have learned that the High Trestle Trail Bridge is one of the largest trail bridges in the world.*

- I wonder why...
    - *I wonder why the state flower is the wild prairie rose.*
    - *I wonder why there are castles in Ida Grove.*

After Reading:

- What did I learn about Iowa?
    - *I have learned that there is a tulip festival in Pella.*
    - *I have learned that the state bird is the eastern goldfinch.*

- Read the book again and look for the glossary words.
    - *I see the word **capital** on page 6, and the word **quarterback** on page 18. The other glossary words are found on pages 22 and 23.*

IOWA
Hi! My name is Ollie. Welcome to Iowa!

I live in Pella. My town is so pretty that it looks like it’s from a fairy tale.

Every May, Pella has a **festival** called Tulip Time. It's my favorite time of year.

Iowa is in the **midwestern** United States. The **capital** is Des Moines.

Fun Fact: Des Moines is the largest city in Iowa.

The state bird is the eastern goldfinch.

The wild prairie rose is the state flower.

We grow a lot of corn in Iowa. Some of it is used to feed animals.

Fun Fact: Iowa is one of the states that **produces** the most corn in the U.S.

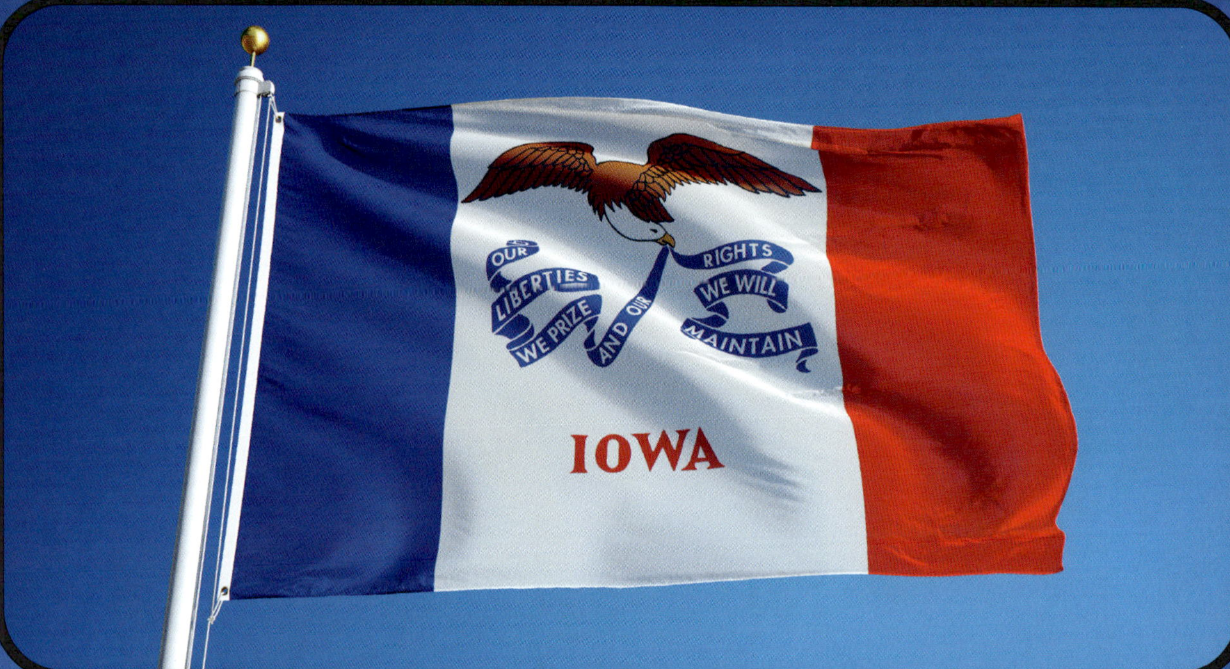

My state flag has a red, white, and blue stripe. In the middle there is an eagle holding a blue ribbon with the state **motto** on it.

The University of Iowa's wrestling team has won 24 national championships.

I like to bike on the High Trestle Trail. The trail is 25 miles (40 km) long.

Fun Fact: The High Trestle Trail Bridge is one of the largest trail bridges in the world.

I enjoy riding the swings at the Iowa State Fair in Des Moines.

The strawberry in Strawberry Point is huge!

Actress Danai Gurira, who played a role in the movie *Black Panther*, was born in Iowa. NFL **quarterback** Joe Burrow was also born in Iowa.

Fun Fact: President Herbert Hoover was born in West Branch, Iowa.

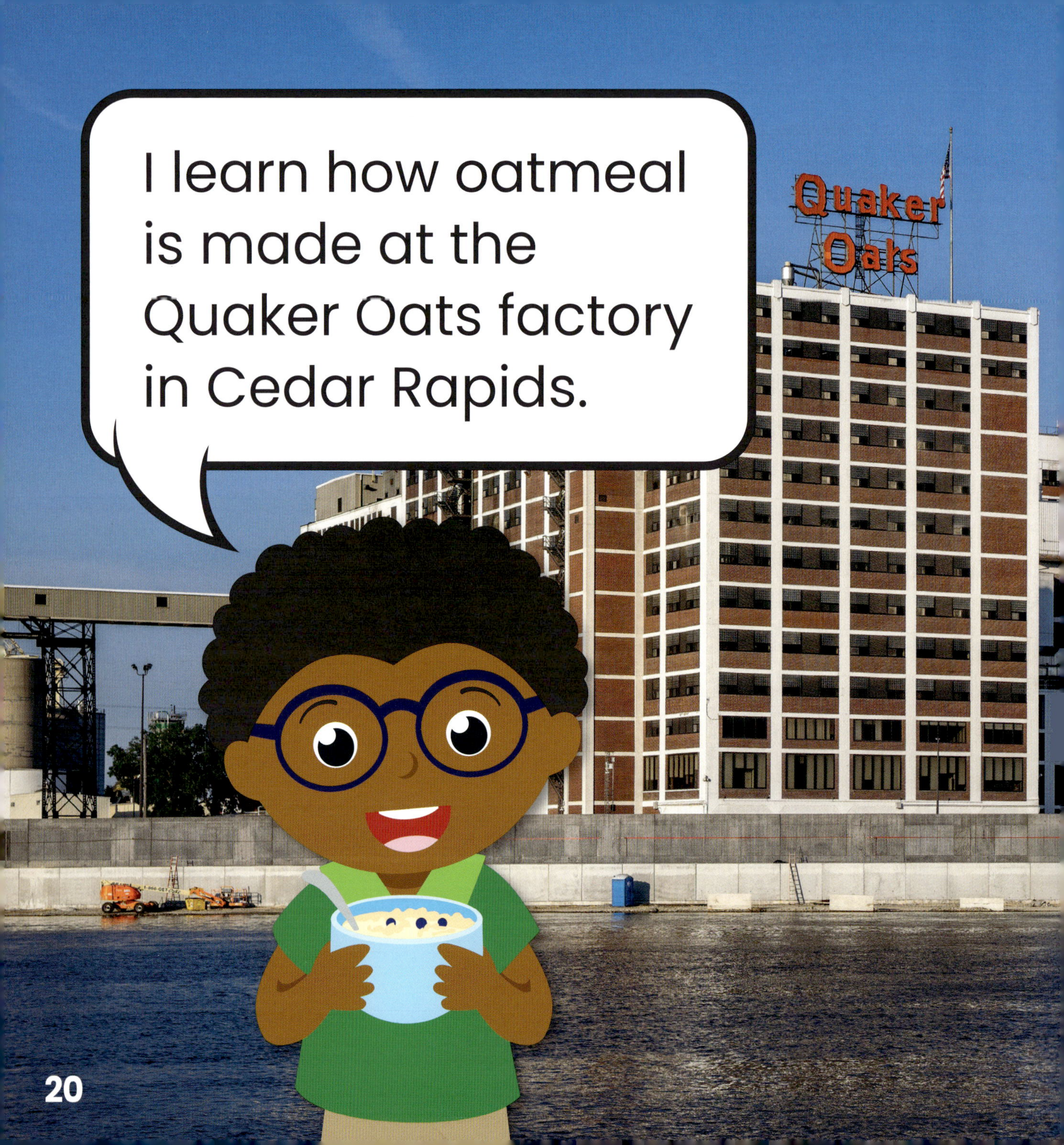

I learn how oatmeal is made at the Quaker Oats factory in Cedar Rapids.

The castles of Ida Grove are pretty.

Glossary

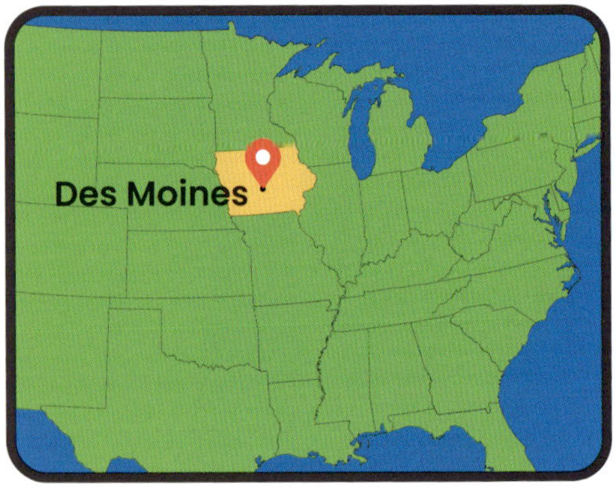

capital (cap-ih-tuhl): The city or town where the government of a country, state, or province is located

festival (fes-tuh-vuhl): An event where people gather to celebrate something

midwestern (mid-west-urn): The northern central part of the United States

motto (mot-oh): A short saying used to describe a belief or rules of behavior

produces (pruh-doos-es): Makes or grows something for sale or use

quarterback (kwor-ter-bak): A position on a football team

Index

About the Author

Christina Earley lives in sunny South Florida with her husband and son. She enjoys traveling around the United States and learning about different historical places. Her hobbies include hiking, yoga, and baking.

Written by: Christina Earley
Designed and Illustrated by: Bobbie Houser
Series Development: James Earley
Proofreader: Melissa Boyce
Educational Consultant: Marie Lemke M.Ed.

Photographs:
Alamy: ZUMA Press, Inc.: p. 13; Carol Dembinsky/Dembinsky Photo Associates: p. 16; Lyroky: p. 17; Serhii Chrucky: p. 20; Hum Images: p. 21
LOC: p. 19
Newscom: Ian Johnson/Icon Sportswire DCD: p. 18 right, 23
Shutterstock: Ralf Broskvar: cover; Lowell Monke: p. 3; Laurens Hoddenbagh: p. 4; Bella Bender: p. 5, 22; Volina: p. 6, 22; f11photo: p. 7; Rabbitti: p. 8; freya-photographer: p. 9; Serg64: p. 10-11; Fotokostic: p. 11, 23; railway fx: p. 12, 23; Life Atlas Photography: p. 14; John Brueske: p. 14-15; DFree: p. 18 left

Crabtree Publishing

crabtreebooks.com 800-387-7650

Printed in the U.S.A./072023/CG20230214

Published in Canada
Crabtree Publishing
616 Welland Avenue
St. Catharines, Ontario
L2M 5V6

Published in the United States
Crabtree Publishing
347 Fifth Avenue
Suite 1402-145
New York, New York, 10016

Library and Archives Canada Cataloguing in Publication
Available at Library and Archives Canada

Library of Congress Cataloging-in-Publication Data
Available at the Library of Congress

Hardcover: 978-1-0398-0514-9
Paperback: 978-1-0398-0546-0
Ebook (pdf): 978-1-0398-0610-8
Epub: 978-1-0398-0578-1